Hippos

Hippos

by Sally M. Walker
photographs by Gerry Ellis
A Carolrhoda Nature Watch Book

Carolrhoda Books, Inc. / Minneapolis

Special thanks to Dr. William Barklow of Framingham College for sharing his vast knowledge of hippos.

Carolrhoda Books, Inc., a division of Lerner Publishing Group
241 First Avenue North, Minneapolis, MN 55401 U.S.A.

Website address: www.lernerbooks.com

Library of Congress Cataloging-in-Publication Data

Walker, Sally M.
    Hippos / by Sally M. Walker ; photographs by Gerry Ellis.
        p.   cm.
        "A Carolrhoda nature watch book."
        Includes index.
        Summary: An introduction to the physical characteristics, habits, and natural environment of the common and the pygmy hippopotamus.
        ISBN 1-57505-078-1 (lib. bdg. : alk. paper)
        1. Hippopotamus—Juvenile literature. 2. Pygmy hippopotamus—Juvenile literature. [1. Hippopotamus.]
    I. Ellis, Gerry, ill.
    II. Title.
    QL737.U57W34 1998
    599.63'5—dc21   96–38135

Manufactured in the United States of America
3 4 5 6 7 8 – JR – 07 06 05 04 03 02

CONTENTS

INTRODUCTION

Like a mirror, the calm surface of a lake in Africa reflects the blue sky and fluffy white clouds. Slowly, two goggly eyes ease out of the water. Next, two nostrils blow a spray of water into the air. Gradually, a gigantic head appears, and an enormous mouth yawns so wide that there is room enough for you to climb inside and sit. Of course, you wouldn't. The long tusks and sharp front teeth send a very clear message: This watering hole is for hippopotamuses, not you!

Hippos seem to have a lot in common with the mud-loving pig (below). But new research suggests they are more closely related to whales (left) and dolphins (bottom).

The hippopotamus is the third largest land mammal in the world; only the elephant and rhinoceros are bigger. Because the name "hippopotamus" is almost as long as the animal, most people call it "hippo" for short. The name comes from two Greek words, *hippos* and *potamos,* which mean "river horse." This might make you think these animals are related to horses, but they are not. For a long time, scientists have believed that hippos were related to pigs. But new studies of hippo genes (the tiny structures in living things that determine characteristics such as size and color) have yielded some surprising news. Hippos' closest relatives may be dolphins and whales!

To try to figure out how long hippo species have existed, scientists look at the **fossil** record. Fossils are animal or plant remains that, over thousands of years, have slowly turned into stone. The fossil record is a collection of all the information on each species that has been gathered from fossils around the world.

Tracing a family tree through the fossil record is not always easy. Like pieces of a large puzzle that have been scattered around your home for months, pieces of the fossil record are frequently missing. That makes it difficult to tell exactly when a species, or group of animals, first existed. But based on fossil evidence, scientists believe that the anthracotheres, a group of mammals that lived about 25 million years ago, are the immediate ancestors of modern hippos.

Ten thousand to forty thousand years ago, many species of hippos roamed throughout Asia, Africa, and central Europe. Although hippos were common and widespread then, only two species are still alive: the common hippo and the pygmy hippo. Both species are found only in Africa, south of the Sahara Desert. And both species are struggling to survive.

Scientists have found remains of an extinct hippo species, Hippopotamus gorgops, *with eyes that bulge even more than a common hippo's.*

The common hippo loves company—and the water. This is the hippo species most often seen in zoos.

The common hippo *(Hippopotamus amphibius)* spends much of its time in shallow water, so it usually lives near rivers or lakes. However, it does not mind the salty water of ocean lagoons, either. About 157,000 of these huge hippos are left in the wild, mostly in open areas in eastern Zaire, Zambia, Malawi, Mozambique, and Zimbabwe.

The pygmy hippo *(Choeropsis liberiensis)* is found mostly in Liberia; a few live in Sierra Leone, Guinea, and the Ivory Coast. Unlike common hippos, pygmy hippos prefer forested areas. These shy creatures spend their days hidden in rivers and swamps that are overhung with shrubs and trees. With increasing speed, these forests are being cleared to make room for farms. For this reason, pygmy hippos are in far more danger of **extinction** (the death of all members of the species) than common hippos. The exact number of pygmy hippos isn't known, but zoologists estimate there are probably only 2,000 in the wild. Another 350 live in zoos around the world. Because pygmy hippos are hard to locate in the wild, most of what we know about them has been learned by studying the zoo animals. There is still a lot more to learn.

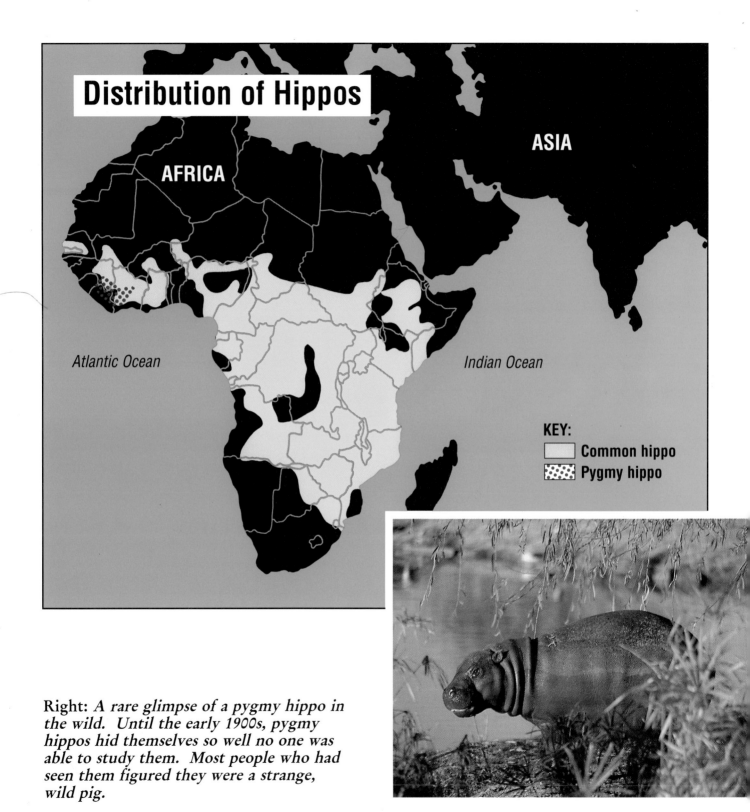

Distribution of Hippos

ASIA

AFRICA

Atlantic Ocean

Indian Ocean

KEY:
Common hippo
Pygmy hippo

Right: *A rare glimpse of a pygmy hippo in the wild. Until the early 1900s, pygmy hippos hid themselves so well no one was able to study them. Most people who had seen them figured they were a strange, wild pig.*

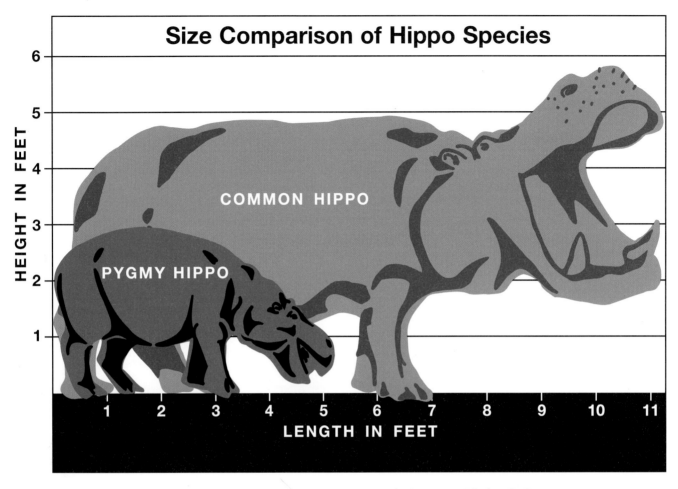

Size Comparison of Hippo Species

HEIGHT IN FEET

COMMON HIPPO

PYGMY HIPPO

LENGTH IN FEET

PHYSICAL CHARACTERISTICS

Common hippos are much larger than pygmy hippos. The males of both species, called **bulls,** are larger than the females, or **cows.** Common hippo bulls are about 4.5 to 5.5 feet tall (1.4–1.7 m) at the shoulder and are about 11.5 feet long (3.5 m). They weigh between 3,500 and 7,000 pounds (1,589–3,178 kg), although some very large bulls can reach 8,000 pounds (3,632 kg). In height and length, cows are several inches shorter than bulls, and they generally weigh between 1,500 and 5,100 pounds (681–2,315 kg).

Compared to common hippos, pygmy hippos seem tiny. They measure 30 to 39 inches tall (76–99 cm) at the shoulder and average 5 feet in length (1.5 m). They are seldom heavier than 500 pounds (227 kg)—about the size of a large hog.

The pygmy hippo (right) *is smaller and sleeker than the common hippo* (below).

At a quick glance, you might think that size is the only difference between the two hippo species. But they are different in several other ways as well. The common hippo has a barrel-shaped body and short, stocky legs. The short legs do not raise its body very far off the ground, and often its belly scrapes along the ground as it moves, leaving behind a shallow trench between the right and left footprints.

Also, the common hippo has a very large head. It can make up almost one-third of a hippo's length and weigh almost 1,000 pounds (454 kg)—that's about as heavy as a dozen fifth graders. The muscles in a hippo's short, thick neck have to be very strong to support the heavy head.

In contrast, the pygmy hippo's body is shaped more like a torpedo—long and slender—and its legs are much slimmer and longer in relation to its body size. A pygmy hippo's head is smaller, and its neck is less chunky.

Just as the common hippo's head (top) *is designed for hanging out in the water, the pygmy hippo's head* (bottom) *is well suited to life on land.*

The eyes and nostrils are also placed differently in the two species. On a common hippo's head, the ears, eyes, and nostrils are level with each other, along the top of the head. This way, a common hippo resting under the water needs to rise only a few inches to be able to hear, see, and breathe. A pygmy hippo's eyes are located more on the sides of the head, which helps the hippo see both ahead and to the side as it wanders through the forest. Its nostrils are positioned lower on its muzzle than a common hippo's, probably because it does not spend as much time underwater.

Still, both species spend time in the water to escape the African heat. When they dive, they fold their ears against their heads. At the same time, both the common hippo's narrow nostrils and the pygmy hippo's rounder ones close tightly. The nostrils remain closed as long as the hippo is underwater—about 20 seconds at a time for young **calves** and about 5 minutes for full-grown adults. When they surface, they snort to blow water away from their nostrils and shake their ears to dry them.

Thick, wrinkly skin is a trademark of hippos. Underneath the skin, a layer of fat protects them from heat and cold, and helps them float. Hippos have very little hair on their bodies, except around their ears and at the ends of their tails. They also have whiskers and eyelashes.

Both hippo species have thick, wrinkly skin, a feature they share with a group of animals called **pachyderms**. Elephants and rhinoceroses belong to this group as well. The name comes from two Greek words, *pachys* and *derma*, which mean "thick skin." The skin in some areas of the body, such as the chest and neck, is particularly thick. These areas are important targets for **predators** such as hyenas, lions, and crocodiles, who kill and eat calves and sick adult hippos. The common hippo's skin may be as thick as 2 inches (5 cm) in these exposed areas. Hippos have rolls of skin around their necks and near the tops of their legs. A layer of fat lies beneath the skin in both species. Common hippos may appear grayish brown or grayish purple on top, and their undersides are usually pink. Pygmy hippos are darker—almost black on top, sometimes with a greenish tinge. Underneath they are grayish yellow or cream colored.

The dark-colored droplets on this common hippo's forehead and snout help protect the animal from sunburn and infections.

Years ago, people believed that hippos could sweat blood. Such a mistake is understandable and also easily explained. Hippos have glands under their skin that produce a salty, oily, reddish brown liquid. This liquid, which in some light looks a little bit like blood, seeps out of the skin to keep it moist, an important protection against the hot sun. The red liquid may also kill germs and help skin wounds heal.

A hippo's toes spread apart to give the large animal better balance and stability.

With a body the size of a hippo's, it is important to have strong legs and firm footing. Each of a hippo's large, rounded feet has four toes. This is a feature of a group of hoofed mammals called even-toed ungulates (UNG-gyoo-lits). Camels, giraffes, deer, and pigs are also members of this group. But unlike the feet of these other even-toed ungulates, hippo toes are connected by stretchy skin, giving them a webbed appearance. Webbed feet help a hippo push its way along in the water more efficiently than it could if the toes were not connected. A pygmy hippo's toes have less webbing than a common hippo's, probably because it spends more time on land.

When a hippo takes a step, its toes spread out flat on the ground. Each one receives a share of the animal's weight. A pygmy hippo's toes spread out more than a common hippo's do. This gives it better balance as it moves over uneven, forest-covered ground. In both species, a pad on the bottom of each foot acts like a cushion and softens the impact of heavy hippo footsteps.

Despite hippos' bulky bodies, steep riverbanks are no obstacle for them.

In spite of their clumsy-looking bodies, hippos can spin around rapidly and climb steep riverbanks. If they need to, they can even gallop at speeds up to 30 miles per hour (48 km/h) for short distances. For longer distances, they resort to a choppy, ground-covering trot. When hippos encounter obstacles, they don't jump over them; they either push them aside or go around.

The premolars (1) and molars (2) are used for chewing. The incisors (3) and canines (4) help the hippo defend itself.

Biologists don't think it is likely that hippos have sharp eyesight. The murky water they live in limits how far they can see, so even if they had good vision, they wouldn't be able to see much anyway. But at night, hippos can see in the dark well enough to wander about on land looking for food.

Hippos are **herbivores,** animals who eat only plants. Most of the common hippo's 42 to 44 teeth and the pygmy hippo's 38 teeth are used for chewing. The hippo's 28 **premolars** and **molars,** the wide, ridged teeth on the sides and in the back of its mouth, mash and grind up the food before it is swallowed.

The hippo's **incisors** (sharp front teeth) and **canine teeth** (tusks) are used only for protection. These teeth grow throughout a hippo's life. Molars, however, do not keep growing. To help them last, molars have a hard covering called enamel. (Human teeth do, too.) But constant grinding does wear down teeth. If the molars become too worn, a hippo can't eat and will starve.

After a hippo swallows, the food travels down to its stomach. There, the nutrients from the food are absorbed, and whatever is left is passed out as **feces,** or solid waste. A hippo's diet contains a lot of cellulose, material that makes up the woody parts of plants. The large amount of cellulose remaining after digestion causes hippos to produce large amounts of solid waste.

Biologist Mike Fredrickson hauls an underwater microphone toward a research site on the Ruaha River in Tanzania.

COMMUNICATION

Whether feeding on land or resting in the water, hippos communicate with a number of sounds that range widely from high-pitched squeaks to deep, thunderous bass notes. Dr. William Barklow, a biologist, and some of his associates have spent years listening to common hippos and recording their sounds.

Using special underwater microphones, the biologists heard sounds similar to the clicks that dolphins and whales make. (As far as biologists know, hippo clicks are used only to communicate and not to determine location, as dolphin and whale clicks are.) The biologists also heard fluttery sounds (like the noise you can make if you stick out your tongue and blow) and underwater bellows that were loud enough to make them cover their ears.

As the scientists recorded these sounds, they realized something very interesting: Some of the loudest underwater bellows were not heard by people standing on the riverbank nearby. Yet other sounds recorded below the surface *were* heard on land. How do hippos do that?

A common hippo can send messages whether its head is in or out of the water.

Sound waves in the air cannot travel into water (they bounce off the water's surface), and sound waves in water do not travel up into the air. Therefore, the researchers knew that sounds heard in both places had to come from two places in the common hippo's body: one above the water's surface, and one below.

Out-of-the-water sounds are made two ways: they can be hummed out through either the hippo's nostrils or its mouth. Underwater sounds start in the hippo's **larynx,** or voice box. They travel through the fatty roll of skin and muscle on the hippo's throat, and pass into the water. With these options, bathing hippos can communicate beneath the water without making a sound above the surface, or they can broadcast to both places at once.

Dr. Barklow also found that common hippos can tell the direction from which an underwater sound comes. If you were to close your eyes and duck underwater while a friend clicked two stones together beneath the surface, you would hear the sound but you could not tell which direction it came from. In water, our ears prevent us from pinpointing the source of the sound.

But hippos have a special way of hearing underwater sounds. The sounds pass through a hippo's jaws and go directly into its inner ears, where sound is sensed. Hippos can tell a sound's location by comparing the sound levels absorbed by their right and left jaws. If the sound from the left side is louder than that from the right side, they know the sound came from its left. Determining a sound's location this way is probably helpful, considering how difficult it is to see through the cloudy water where hippos like to lounge.

MATING TERRITORIES

Recognizing sounds and their sources keeps a common hippo bull aware of who is close by—particularly other bulls who may be wandering into his mating **territory.**

Bulls stake their territories along riverbanks. The **dominant,** or strongest, bulls get to establish their territories in the nicest places—those with easy access to the water and closest to females. Younger, weaker bulls establish their territories farther away. A younger bull must fight and defeat an older bull in order to win a better territory. Females seldom fight, unless they are protecting their young. But when it is necessary, they are tough fighters, so you had better keep your distance.

Common hippo bulls seek out territories as close as they can to the nicest watering holes, where females are bound to gather.

Bulls of both species will fight viciously to protect their mating territories from intruders. But unless a bull is challenged for his territory, he does not usually seek to start fights. In fact, the way a bull marks his territory sends a very clear message to would-be trespassers. He rapidly switches his tail as he produces feces.

The flipping action scatters the waste matter (and the bull's scent) for several yards around, stating definitely, "Someone lives here!" This makes the area rather messy, but it is normal for hippos and does not bother them at all. However, zookeepers find it extremely difficult to keep hippo pens looking clean. Females rarely perform this kind of territorial marking and do not mind it when other hippos cross their paths.

Both in and out of the water, a common hippo bull marks his territory with feces.

Dominant bulls usually tolerate other bulls in their territories as long as the intruders acknowledge who is boss. Hippo fights, which most often take place in or near the water, can last up to several hours, and they are very bloody. So when a bull strays into another bull's territory, he is first given a warning: a wide "yawn" that shows off the angry bull's sharp canine teeth.

The two bulls yawn like this at each other, each time more widely. They may also lunge at each other. But unless the intruder intends to challenge for territory, he backs down and retreats. If the intruder refuses to retreat, the two bulls may scoop up water in their mouths and toss it at each other. Then the two bulls run headlong at each other, mouths open wide. Growling, honking, roaring, and snorting accompany the fight.

Bulls' canine teeth are valuable weapons for slashing at each other's front legs. A common hippo's canines often grow as long as 20 inches (51 cm). The largest modern hippo canine tooth recorded is 25.5 inches (65 cm). These tusks can cause real problems for a victim.

This is no normal yawn. It means "Stay away!"

Common hippo fights are so violent that frequently one of the bulls dies as a result of his injuries.

Standing head to tail, the two bulls continue to bite and batter one another until one of them surrenders, retreats, or is killed. Many deep wounds are inflicted during a fight, and the skin of older hippos is often crisscrossed with scars. It is not unusual for one of the fighters to end up bleeding to death. If a bull is wounded so badly that he is unable to stand, he will likely starve.

A bull may hold the same territory for a few months or, if the area is not disturbed by drought or people, for several years. One bull in Uganda defended the same territory for more than 12 years.

LIFE CYCLE

The bull with the best territory also has the most opportunities for mating, because cows do not look far for a mate. Cows of both species are usually about 3 to 4 years of age when they first come into **estrus,** the time when they can mate and become pregnant. However, they often don't breed until they are several years older. Males are able to breed by the time they are about 5 years old. But because they must compete against dominant bulls, most males don't mate until they are a few years older.

Common hippos in the wild usually come into estrus at the end of the two dry seasons, in February and August. There is a very good reason for this: when the calves are born about 8 months later, one of the two rainy seasons will be in full swing. At these times of year, an ample food supply is available for cows and their calves.

Mating occurs in shallow water.

Biologists do not know how a cow chooses the bull she mates with, but a common hippo cow in estrus often makes a huffing sound, which attracts the attention of nearby bulls. No one has witnessed pygmy hippos mating in the wild. But among pygmy hippos in zoos, a cow does not do anything to get a bull's attention—he seems to know when she is in estrus. He remains close by and sometimes smacks his lips.

Mating itself occurs in shallow water. The cow may move away from the bull three or four times before she lets him mount her. After mating, the cow and bull do not stay together. The next time the cow is in estrus, she may choose either the same bull or a different one. Cows seem to prefer to mate with dominant bulls, rejecting younger or less dominant bulls.

A pygmy calf rests in its mother's shadow.

The calf develops inside its mother for about 7 to 8 months. Just before giving birth, the cow becomes restless and moves to a private place where she can give birth alone. Common hippos are born in the water, and the calf seems to know instinctively (without being taught) how to get to the surface for its first breath of air. Pygmy hippo calves do not instinctively head for the surface, and they sometimes drown when they are born in the water. For that reason, zookeepers keep pygmy hippo cows out of water when they are ready to give birth.

Newborn calves seem tiny when compared to their mothers. Common calves range from 50 to 100 pounds (23–45 kg) and are about 3 feet long (0.9 m) and 1.5 feet tall (0.5 m). Pygmy calves weigh 6 to 14 pounds (2.7–6.4 kg) and are about 1 foot (0.3 m) long. Within several minutes of birth, calves of both species are able to walk.

Shortly after birth, the calf nuzzles around its mother's body until it finds one of her two nipples and begins to nurse. Something very interesting happens when common hippo calves nurse. While they are sucking, their ears fold against their heads and their nostrils close tightly—even when they are nursing on land. They must stop breathing to nurse. Since calves often nurse underwater, closing the ears and nose keeps water from getting in and causing harm.

In common hippo calves, this shutting happens on its own and is not something they must learn. Pygmy calves, however, must learn this. Until they do, they nurse on land. All calves frequently nurse underwater and pop to the surface every few seconds to breathe.

At about 4 months old, calves begin to add plants to their diet, and by about 8 months, they eat only solid food. During these early months, calves gain weight rapidly—about 10 pounds per day (4.5 kg) for common hippo calves and about 1 pound per day (0.5 kg) for pygmy calves.

For the first few weeks after birth, a common hippo calf and its mother remain alone. (Pygmy hippos are almost always on their own.) When common hippos return to the **herd,** or group of hippos to which they belong, the cow and calf become members of the **crèche** (KRESH), a kind of hippo nursery school. The crèche is located in an area close to water, where hippos feel safe. There, calves play with other hippos their age. The females often play hide-and-seek games, while the males tend to fight mock battles. All baby hippos like to roll around in the water.

These male common hippo calves are just playing, but such games help them build strong muscles and determine dominance. When they are about a year old, they will leave the herd and seek out territories of their own, usually away from those of older, stronger bulls.

Cows share the job of baby-sitting for the crèche's young. Taking turns, one or two mothers, or **aunts,** stay near the calves and keep a lookout for danger—predators who will eat a hippo calf. Meanwhile, the other mothers are free to leave the crèche and go about their daily business.

In addition to guarding against predators, the aunts watch out for wandering bulls who might accidentally crush a calf. A bull in an irritable mood might even attack a baby hippo. A quiet bull who behaves himself properly may be allowed into the crèche. But if he becomes rowdy, the cows will chase him away.

Although this common hippo calf has grown a lot since birth, it still needs the protection of the cows in its herd.

Hippo mothers are very protective of their babies. They are also strict about how they expect a calf to behave. When outside of the crèche, common hippo calves stay close to their mothers. They often climb up on their mothers' backs and bound off, playing a hippo variation of king of the hill. If danger threatens, a cow can easily protect her calf by placing her body between it and a predator.

At times, a cow may have several of her calves living with her. (Female calves often remain with their mothers until they are fully grown, possibly as long as 4 years. A male calf may leave when he is as young as 1 year.) On the way to grazing areas, calves form a line behind their mother according to age. The youngest calf walks closest to the cow, and the oldest takes up the rear.

In or out of the water, a calf stays close to its mother.

A cow who is angry with her calf is not shy about letting the youngster know it. When a calf does not pay attention or refuses to obey, its mother nudges it with her head. Continued misbehavior earns a harsh nip or even a bonk from the cow's head that can be hard enough to knock a calf off its feet.

Cows and calves show their affection for each other by nuzzling and licking. They also lightly scrape each other's skin with their canine teeth. This feels good to them in much the same way a back-scratch feels good to you.

Healthy cows are able to give birth every 2 to 3 years until they reach old age. Both species of hippo can live about 30 to 35 years in the wild, but because of human hunters, many of them do not live that long. In zoos, hippos often live to be over 40 years old.

DAILY ROUTINE

Adult pygmy hippos prefer to remain alone and do not form herds. A cow and her calf will stay together, but bulls do not like to be in groups. In zoos, pygmy hippos become irritated and angry if they are forced to be too close to one another. In contrast, common hippos don't seem to mind each other's company. Their herds usually contain between five and one hundred individuals.

A pygmy hippo becomes irritated if people or other hippos get too close.

A herd of common hippos naps in the sun.

Common hippo herds spend most of their time resting. (Shifting a huge body around isn't easy!) Up to 86 percent of their day is spent underwater. Often all you can see sticking out are eyes and nostrils. A sleeping hippo rises to the surface every few minutes, breathes out, takes another breath, and then sinks again. This action is not something a hippo needs to think about—it is as automatic as blinking is to humans.

Slow-moving or still waters a few feet deep are favorite napping areas for common hippos. In these places, they can stand on the bottom rather than having to swim. Calves find this easier, too, since they do not have to swim and nurse at the same time. Hippos avoid swift currents since they are likely to be pushed off their feet and swept away—something unpleasant at any size, but not made any easier by a hippo's bulk.

Whenever possible, hippos stay close to water so they have a place to hide when they are frightened. Pygmy hippos reach the water through the winding tunnels they have made through the thick forest. They also hide in the forest undergrowth.

Despite the amount of time hippos spend in the water, they are not very graceful swimmers. Still, their strokes enable them to move quickly through the water—much faster than a person can paddle a boat or swim. Years ago, people did not know how hippos managed to move so quickly underwater. Daring photographers provided the answer by filming hippos beneath the water. This is a dangerous task, because a hippo may attack if it thinks the photographer is threatening it. A hippo's bite is strong enough to kill a person, and an attacking hippo can gouge a boat with its tusks and crush or tip a boat with its body.

When a hippo moves through deep water, it pushes off the bottom with its hind legs and heads up toward the surface. The hippo tucks its hind legs up close to its body so its balloon shape will glide more easily through the water. When it sinks back to the bottom, the hippo lands first on its front legs. After all four legs are down, the hippo is ready to push off again. Biologists call this kind of swimming **punting**. Although it is ungainly on land, a punting hippo looks as if it were dancing on tiptoe on the river bottom, except that it may be able to reach speeds of 20 miles per hour (32 km/h)!

A punting common hippo touches bottom with its front feet first.

Hippos do not rest in water because they are lazy. Unlike humans, they have no sweat glands. Hanging out in the water is an easy way to keep their skin cool and moist. Like the heat, insects are a constant irritation. Fortunately, hippos and mud are seldom far apart. When a hippo **wallows,** or rolls around in the mud, a muddy shield is left on the skin that helps prevent bugs from biting.

A cattle egret finds a meal on a wallowing common hippo.

While lounging in the water, hippos provide a service to the community of plants and animals that live there. A hippo's feces are a source of food for algae and microscopic plants. In turn, fish nibble on the plants, and other animals eat the fish. A hippo's feet also stir up the mud on the bottom of the river or lake. The bottom-dwelling creatures tossed up with the mud are tasty meals for fish and other creatures. Catfish and sucker fish do hippos a favor in return.

They clean the hippo's skin by eating algae and other materials that have collected on it. Hippos also open their mouths wide and let the fish swim in and pick food from around their molars.

A hippo also has bird friends to help keep its skin clean. The oxpecker picks off ticks and other parasites that dine on the hippo's blood. Cattle egrets, geese, and other water birds often perch on the backs of hippos resting in the water and eat the insects they find there.

At twilight, common hippos head for dry land and their feeding grounds. Although they may nibble on water plants while they wallow, these plants are not the animals' main source of food.

About 2 hours before sunset, common hippos rouse from their sleepy day. This is their most active time of day and is when most vocalizing occurs. It is also when calves do most of their playing and when mating occurs. Then, as twilight arrives, the hippos lumber out of the water and trudge up the riverbank and through the grass to their feeding areas. Over time, they wear deep ruts in the ground. Within a mile or two of the watering hole, each hippo branches off onto a path that leads to its own private feeding area. Scattered feces from earlier feeding trips help the hippo know it is traveling along the correct trail.

Hippos in the wild pluck grass, their favorite food, with their lips. Like walking lawn mowers, they waddle along, moving their heads from side to side and tearing off mouthfuls of grass. The grassy areas where hippos graze are closely cut, as if they have been mown. For this reason, people sometimes call these areas "hippo lawns." Hippos also eat tender shoots and leaves, and fruit that has fallen from trees. Zoo hippos are fed about 100 pounds (45 kg) of vegetables, hay, and grains each day.

Except for cows who have calves with them, hippos usually graze alone. They spend most of the night grazing (although they sometimes lie down for a nap) and may wander from 3 to 6 miles (5–10 km) within their feeding areas. Dawn's approach signals to hippos that it is time to head back to the water and the daytime safety of their wallowing areas.

Zoologists who have watched common hippos in the wild report that herds tend to remain in the same area as long as water levels remain about the same. When water levels in water holes and rivers drop during droughts, hippos are forced to seek new homes.

This carving from the wall of an ancient Egyptian tomb shows hunters killing hippos and other river creatures.

HIPPOS AND PEOPLE

Although calves and sick or old adult hippos may be attacked by animal predators, generally a hippo's worst enemies are people. Throughout history, humans have hunted hippos for their meat and for sport. The walls of many Egyptian tombs have drawings of people hunting hippos. At one time, thousands of hippos lived along Egypt's Nile River. However, Europeans who visited or settled in Egypt in the 1700s and 1800s were eager hippo hunters, and there are no longer any wild hippos left in that country.

Hippos play their own part in their violent relationship with humans by killing about three hundred people each year. Many of these deaths could be avoided if people—especially boaters—would watch out for hippos. It is never a good idea to get between a cow and her young, or any hippo and the water. But even in situations in which hippos are the attackers, they may still end up the losers: humans who have survived a hippo attack have been known to strike back and kill their attacker.

During the past one hundred years, people have been using more of Africa's land for farming. Wet places where common hippos naturally live are also good for growing rice. Grazing hippos often invade rice paddies, destroying the farmer's crop and source of income. The forests of Liberia, the pygmy hippo's natural habitat, are being cut for farmland and wood. Although there are some pygmy hippos in zoos, those in the wild could face extinction if their habitat is not protected. In particular, areas need to be set aside where hippos can roam freely and safely.

Much of Liberia has been cleared of trees to make room for plantations and farms.

A ban on the sale of products made from elephant ivory has made this common hippo tooth very valuable.

The newest threat to hippos is **poachers,** or illegal hunters, who kill the animals for their teeth. The hard, white substance that forms hippo and elephant tusks is called **ivory.** Throughout history, people have carved ivory into decorative objects such as jewelry, umbrella handles, and sculptures. Dentists used to make false teeth out of hippo ivory because it does not turn yellow.

Elephants were hunted for their ivory until they nearly became extinct. A worldwide ban on buying and selling elephant ivory has discouraged some poachers from killing them. Yet steady demand for ivory trinkets makes it worthwhile for the poachers to continue, and more of them have turned to hippos for their livelihood.

A large herd of wallowing hippos is unfortunately an easy target for a poacher with a gun. The declining numbers of both pygmy and common hippos has attracted the attention of conservationists (people who want to protect wildlife). The Convention on International Trade in Endangered Species (CITES) lists pygmy hippos as an **endangered** species and has banned trade in the animals or any products made from them. Trade in common hippos is not banned, but international laws limit trade in an attempt to keep the population stable. These are only the first steps toward saving hippos. Educating people about these animals and the way they live is another. If the number of common hippos continues to drop, perhaps a ban on trading the ivory of common hippos will be necessary to save the species.

Watching hippos in zoos can be fun and interesting, but those in the wild play an important role in the ecosystems, or communities of plants and animals, to which they belong. If hippos, like elephants, are hunted close to extinction, these ecosystems will be affected in ways we may not be able to predict. It is up to us to make sure these large and fascinating animals survive.

GLOSSARY

aunt: a mother hippo who helps watch over other hippos' calves. She may or may not be related.

bull: an adult male hippo

calves: baby hippos

canine teeth: large, sharp tusks in the front of a hippo's mouth that are used for fighting

cow: an adult female hippo

crèche: the protected area near the water's edge where common hippo calves and their mothers live

dominant: the strongest male in an area

endangered: at risk of losing all members of a species forever

estrus: the period during which a female hippo is able to become pregnant

extinction: the death of all members of a species

feces: solid waste matter

fossil: plant or animal remains that have been preserved in stone

herbivore: any animal that eats only plants

herd: a group of adult and young common hippos who live together in the same area

incisors: sharp front teeth that are used for fighting

ivory: a hard, white substance that forms the tusks (canines) of hippos and elephants

larynx: the part of the throat that is used to make sounds

molars: large, ridged back teeth that are used for grinding food

pachyderms: large, thick-skinned, hoofed mammals such as the hippopotamus, the rhinoceros, and the elephant

poachers: people who illegally hunt animals

predator: an animal who hunts another animal for food

premolars: side teeth, between the canines and the molars, that are used for grinding food

punting: moving through the water by pushing off the bottom while tucking in the legs

territory: the area a bull claims and defends as his own for mating purposes

wallow: to roll about or rest in a damp, muddy place

INDEX

All photos courtesy of Gerry Ellis except: © Brandon D. Cole/ENP Images, p. 6 (top); © David Lorenz Winston/ENP Images, p. 6 (center); © Konrad Wothe/ENP Images, pp. 6 (bottom), 19, 22; © Erwin and Peggy Bauer, pp. 9 (inset), 33; Frank S. Todd/EarthViews, p. 11 (top); © Frank B. Balthis, p. 12 (bottom); Art Wolfe, p. 14; © Bill Sciallo, p. 15; Daniel J. Cox/NATURAL EXPOSURES, pp. 16, 29; © Ron Kimball, pp. 17, 32; William Barklow, p. 18; © Pete Oxford/ENP Images, p. 23; © Michele Burgess, p. 24; © Michael M. Fairchild, p. 27; © Paul H. Kuiper/ENP Images, p. 40; © Eric Miller/Panos Pictures, p. 41; © J. Short/TRIP Photographic Library, p. 42; © Brian Vikander, p. 43. Illustrations on pp. 7, 9, 10 by John Erste © Carolrhoda Books.

ABOUT THE AUTHOR

Sally M. Walker is the author of numerous science books for children, including *Earthquakes* (a 1997 Outstanding Science Trade Book for Children) and *Rhinos,* both published by Carolrhoda Books. Although her favorite job is writing, Ms. Walker also works as a children's literature consultant and has taught children's literature at Northern Illinois University. While she writes, Ms. Walker is usually surrounded by her family's golden retriever and two cats, who don't say very much but provide good company. She lives in Illinois with her husband and two children.

ABOUT THE PHOTOGRAPHER

Gerry Ellis has explored the world as a professional photographer and naturalist for nearly two decades. His images of wildlife and natural landscapes have won him many awards, including several honors in the BBC Wildlife Photographer of the Year competition. Among his many publications are two other Carolrhoda Nature Watch titles, *Cheetahs* and *Rhinos.* Mr. Ellis lives in Portland, Oregon.